TRANQUILITY OF MIND

EMBRACE THE PRESENT

MARIAM FRANCIS

Made with ❤ on the BookLeaf Publishing Platform
www.bookleafpub.in
www.bookleafpub.com

Dedication

To the restless hearts seeking peace.

To the wanderers searching for stillness and to those
who find solace in words.

This collection is for y'all.

May these poems be a gentle companion, guiding you
toward the tranquility, you've always carried within.

Preface

Tranquility of Mind is a journey into the depths of stillness, a quiet rebellion against the chaos that surrounds us. In this collection, words are woven into an invitation to pause, to reflect, and to rediscover the serenity that resides within.

Each poem is a whisper, a gentle nudge toward finding solace amidst life's clamor. They are moments captured in verse, born from the ebb and flow of emotions, from the quest for clarity in the storm of thoughts, and from the endless search for peace in a restless world.

This book is not merely a collection of poetry; it is a sanctuary. It speaks to the weary, the dreamers, and the seekers, offering them a space to breathe and be. Through its pages, may you find a companion in your quiet hours, a mirror to your innermost feelings, and a bridge to your own tranquility of mind.

Acknowledgements

The 'Tranquility of Mind' is an anthology of conscious courage and embracing the changes in one's life, self composed. As life is like a roller coaster, enjoy and nurture with the living present.

Gratitude to athe almighty and to all those, who encouraged me and their thoughtful feedback were the fuel that kept me going. I present a sincere gratitude to my family, especially my husband, for his love and boosterism. To all my mentors, who were part and parcel of my writing journey, thank you for your guidance, insight and for always pushing me to refine my craft.

I am profoundly grateful to my readers and fellow writers, whose love for poetry reminds me of the beauty in shared words. Finally, this book is dedicated to all those who find solace in poetry. May of these verses offer you comfort, reflection and joy.

With love and gratitude,
Mariam Francis.

1. Embrace the Present

1

Paint your world with a beautiful terrain,
Summering with a fist full of grain.
Look around with transparency to sow,
the yearning seeds in line of how.
Which Lingers like a jack into one's life voyage,
like a yielding field preparing for soyage.
Needed to unruffle and overcome all the struggles.
Because as the time passes the morosely mind,
becomes like a barren land.
Therefore, embracing the present is necessary,
Just like taking meticulous care of an agrarian field is
necessary.

2. Fortune

What you view or happens...
may or may not be superstitious ,
but it can be superfluous in your mind.
Just like genetically ancestry, these thoughts slew in our
minds.
With presentiments, just like everyone's perception.
New to analysis. Whether it's true ? Or just a nonsense
point of view.
In life serendipity, some act gusty.
But some live life like a lanty.
We all are smitten to our natal.
Though, we human's are fortunate enough unlike a
wandering cattle.
Every creature's onerous path is shaped up by their
statal.

3. The quality of being graceful is Dexterity

To the vorious me.
To the hilarious me.
I struggle with sinuous in me.
It's not a phasic self in me.
But a person who is emotionally akin in me.
Who breaks all the falouses in me.
To bring out the best in me.

4. Resilience

Viciousness in the silence...,
does not define innate violence,
But Growing up with one's acceptance does.
As Keeping the soul intact to the Earth's surface...,
Making the spirit quest for the scope of Truth..
Who...am I ..? What's the purpose?
These Question, we forget to ask ourselves,
deep into the roots...intangible like an algae in a deep
ocean.
Unable to recognise one's crude nature.
Moving and struggling in a comfortable way back and
forth, assuming through one's lens.
Thus,forward..and forward...and forward..we move..
to connect with one's own self in resilience.

5. Peace

Life is not a bed of roses,
which we smell with our noses.
As in the battlefield of life,
The fights can be countless but still we have to survive.
Freedom from war, is what need,
but unlike a diving bird, we human's are greed.
Avoiding conflicts is not only our goal,
but also maintaining peace, should be one's goal.
Freedom fighters , who fought for our country's
freedom is now just mere commentary.
But our mindset's are still not emancipated.
It's not justice to these patriotic souls.
It has alienated us, all.
They risked their lives, to bring peace to our nation as a
whole.
Therefore, freedom from insecurities is needed, which is
only possible with unity.
Though in reality, the fear is a matter that doubt's our
individual integrity.

6. Happiness

Life's most persistent and urgent question .. is what are
we doing withour life?
Life doesn't comes with a book of instructions ,
it's good to be humble rather than be in a state of
destruction....
As mistakes are the best teachers
that gives a life long experience to human creatures.
For everyone, love is the only deriving force, capable of
transforming even an evil soul.
Forgive as forgiveness is a grateful act, be Stoic , keep no
grudges.
Because life is a blessing , a prudent friend.
Therefore, use your golden tongue to spread the words of
joy and happiness...
and don't feel alone , as god is omnipresent. He is always
there for you, my friend .
So, be happy and keep singing the song of gratitude life
long.
As, the world will be always be critical about you,
whether you do right or wrong.

7. Emotionless

WALKING AWAY FROM THE LOVE OF MY LIFE, I
DIDN'T REALISE THE IMPORTANCE OF HIS JOY,
THOUGHS, ONCE HE WAS MY INSPIRATION .
BUT I WAS LOST I. THE WORLD OF GLAM AND
MISCONCEPTION.
WHAT'S WORNG HAVE I DONE..? WHY NOW I
MORON..?
LIKE EVERYONE I WAS BUSY MAKING MONEY TO
GRATIFY THE NEEDS. STILL I HAVEN'T STATIFIED
MY GREEDS..
HOW LOST I WAS IN THIS WORLD OF BOREDOM.
I COULDN'T EVEN RECOGNISE THE TOUCH OF MY
SON. I BECAME SO, DUMB.
WHAT'S WRONG WITH ME ..? I KNOW HE LOVE'S
ME.
ALL HE WANTED WAS TO LEAN ON ME.

8. What matters?

Looks do matters... really?
Personality do matters.. really?
Standing distinct...do Matters?
..yes..
With Living reality?
...yes ..
Don't forget.... .God created us ..All.
He is above all.
Not the human hierarchy.
And we all are creaters of our OWN living reality....
so, shape it accordingly.
All that Matters to you....by your own sense .... be the
MASTER of your own reality.

9. Praise to the Lord

Namaste or salam,
We all are one under God's command.
Namaskāram or Nomoskar,
Our souls are source of vigor.
Vaṇakkam or Namaskāra,
We all dwell in a Universe, full of love, joy, hope in a
wagara.

10. Our Universe

Our universe comprises of everything that exists in
space...
Just like unity in diversity in India that does not omit
any race.
The Milky way appearing as a white band across the sky
on a clear night...
Just like the pious Ganga, flowing in arms of the Mother
Earth as a river of light.
The family of the sun has serendipity.....
Free from dogma and custom.... With the sun in the
centre of the solar system
and all the eight planets, held together by gravity....
Just like soldiers of a country bound with fierce loyalty.
We praise Earth as a unique matriarchal celestial body
with life.....
Then why patriarchal body dominates our social life.
We say the universe is expanding.. As galaxies are
moving far away from each other..
Just like the surrealism is expanding... The quenching for
humanity is moving away from each one of us.

11. Take control

Why lost?
Worrying about the cost..?
Looking for something like an archy.
But we all are living in dystopia,
With no monarchy...
With no autocracy..
With No dictatorship..
We all are smitten on someone else's authorship.
We plead for an alien monitoring,
frightened to take our life's in our control.
But why what's the fear.
Take the control with chear.

12. WE SHAPE OUR WORLD

FIELDS ARE MANY.. BUT ARE YOU IN ANY..?
WE ACKNOWLEDGE THE MOST INEQUITABLE
PLACES ON THE EARTH,
THOUGH, WE CONSIDER MONEY ARE AS THE MOST
PRECIOUS, HUMAN WEALTH.
WE INTERACTED WITH THE GROUND WASTE OF
SURE.
NOT ACKNOWLEDGING THE TRUTH OF LIFE AT
ALL.
TRANQUILITY OF MIND IS NECESSARY TO EMBRACE
THE PRESENT.
AS, LIFE IS A PRESENT. ....SO, PULL UP YOUR SOCKS
AND BE ALWAYS READY
BECAUSE THIS WORLD'S NASTY FANTASY, WILL
NOT LET YOU BE IN THE CIRCLE OF SOUND ....
UNTILL AND UNLESS, YOU FACE THE WORLD'S
BATTLEGROUND.

13. Love

Love shapes you.
Love nurtures you.
Loves speaks for you.
Love does for you.
Love fights for you.
Love kills for you.
Love steals for you.
Love loses for you.
Love respects for you.
Love cares for you.
Love bliss for you
Love matters for you.
Love is you.

14. The irony of a fake lover

The people who once promised to stay
Turned out to be fake.
The love , they said would be eternal,
Turned out to be mortal.
The pain, they said would heal,
Turned out to be disease.
The tears, they said to wipe off
Turned out to be water fall.
The care , they said will always be there ,
Turned out to be ignorance .
The life , they once said to make beautiful ,
Turned out to be an empty survival .
The happiness became hard
The feelings became hollow
The smile became a struggle
The expectations became disappointments
The loyalty became vague
The expressions became dead
And YET THE LIFE GOES ON.........

15. LET'S HOPE

15

Vinkle thoughts of an unravel mind,
grimes with dark nights.
Rinse away the uncouth and winkle away the goth.
Winkle your mind with manifestation,
don't pokey yourself with manipulation.
Embrace yourself with discretion,
for yourself satisfaction.
Unconstrained, nonjudgmental with the will of
circumspectipn,
cautioning oneself that the world will and will always be
judgmental.
So, wave away such insecurities, live and let live happily.

16. Green

Lushes of nature,
With the help of sun lustre.
Leaves big or small ferns,
Just like marigold leaves foliage turns into dark green.
Swaying in the air is the elegance and romance of the
rose flowers,
along with the dust of musky wood, dotaging on the
face.
Dew of the dawn, heals the wan.
Trumpeting sound of swans,
awakens the sprits of dons.
Chirping of birds,
feels like a melodic gooey in the ears.
Crunch of dead leaves by foot,
brings our eyes back to the roots.

17. Glory

17

The renaissance of time..
Is likely to change after every century.
The appreciation of history,
Is likely to change after every century.
The glory of the rulers,
Is likely to change after every century.
The apocalypse of human culture,
Is likely to change after every century.
Only the glory of the God, almighty,
Remains the same throughout the centuries.

18. Don't worry

18

Everyone is repeating.
Only the faces keep changing.
Shielding with makeup,
In order to cope up.
What for is the extravagance ..
What for is the menace..
Breathe away the worry of opinions
And throw away the people opinions..
Because life finds a way and so, will you.

19. Dare to Dream

19

Do what your heart says.
Not what world wants from you.
Dare to dream.
Don't bother about world's obnoxious scream.
Live and file.
Atleast give it a try.
Fall and rise.
Don't bound yourself with lies.
Open your up your conscience and dare to fly.
As the sky is not the limit.
You have the entire universe to try.

20. Change is inevitable

Everyone changes,
jus the mistakes are not repeating.
As we grow and learn.
But not regret.
Only the faces keep changing.
Don't know what the world is waning.
Shielding with makeup,
In order to cope up.
What for is the extravagance ..
What for is the menace..
Breathe away the worry of opinions
And throw away the people opinions..
Because life finds a way and so, will you.

21. Forget the Past

Take life as an offering, a gift of stillness,
and let the universe verses guide you toward the peace,
you seek .
Without any kind of illness.
Anything in the past that entangles you,
is noticeably not solved.
Feel the emotion consciously that is surfacing from the
external triggers.
Heal yourself from the tiggering thoughts.
Don't you feel lost..
Because there is nothing to be absolved.

www.ingramcontent.com/pod-product-compliance
Lightning Source LLC
LaVergne TN
LVHW050505210726
843509LV00015BA/3005

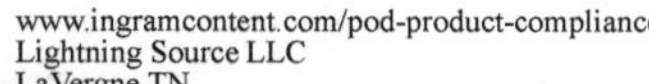